The Dedalus Press

Turn Your Head

Michael O'Dea

Turn Your Head

Michael O'Dea

DUBLIN 2003

The Dedalus Press
24 The Heath ~ Cypress Downs ~ Dublin 6W
Ireland

© Michael O'Dea and The Dedalus Press, 2003

Cover by Michael Cummins

ISBN 1 904556 09 4 (paper)
ISBN 1 904556 10 8 (bound)

ACKNOWLEDGEMENTS
Acknowledgements are due to the editors of *Cyphers, Poetry Ireland Review, West 47, Force 10, Acorn, THE SHOp, Electric Acorn, Rainbows and Stone, De Brakke Hond, Out to Lunch Anthology* and *InCognito* where some of these poems have appeared.

Dedalus Press books are represented and distributed —
in the U.S.A. and Canada by **Dufour Editions Ltd.**, P.O. Box 7, Chester Springs, Pennsylvania 19425 —
in the UK by **Central Books**, 99 Wallis Road, London E9 5LN

The Dedalus Press receives financial assistance from
An Chomhairle Ealaíon, The Arts Council, Ireland.

Printed in Dublin by The Johnswood Press

Contents

The Green Road 7
With You 8
Scarecrows 9
Blue-veined Old Hands 10
Soldier 11
Before the End 12
Armani Stops at Our House 13
The Yellow Rose 14
Legend 15
Coping. Not Coping 16
Screenplay 17
Who Knows 19
Fabulous Arthur Quinn 20
Visit 21
Frost in Dublin 22
Looking for Your Boat 23
Please Turn Your Head Mr Kavanagh 24
Growing Apart 25
Outside Tesco's 26
At Naomh Einne's Well 27
Sure Sight 28
There 29
Then and Now 30
Railway Child 31
Thunder Shower 32
Cruise Missiles 33
Fifteen Irises 34
When You Pass 35
Old Man 36
Revisiting Lough Ree 37

Wish   38
Running Away   39
Those Marches   40
Explorers   42
Angry   43
Trap   44
Snowtime   45
Seeing   46
Suddenly   47
Galileo   48
In Memory of Kathleen   49
Frosty Morning   50
Low   51
Where the Poetry Comes From   52
Moonfire   53
Films in Your Face   54
The Poems are Past   55

Tuol Sleng Still   57

The Green Road

The blackthorns above Fenore
are flight rooted;
they are folklore's skeletons,
beggars of the green road.

Scoured to the knuckle,
stunted on burren karst,
they are the hags on the mountain
hunched from Atlantic gales.

Yet even this stone-weary day,
with hunger perched on their throats,
a robin is singing in each
notes that singe the February air.

Beneath the huddling sky,
into the ear of the green road
it pours, clear as water,
the music of tin whistlers' dreams.

With You

The fields, green with snow
under an apple blue sky;

you, brimming
winter's brightness,

turning cartwheels;
your whole body grinning.

The silver trees of our breathing
in full flower;

my golden happiness
in being with you

till the shafts of shadow
turned purple at sunset;

and our hours together
colourless at parting.

Scarecrows

We are two scarecrows: rags and string;
what the rain softens the wind picks clean.

We are two scarecrows: sticks and straw;
crows fly out from underneath our jackets.

We are two scarecrows: nails and wire;
each day drowning as the corn grows higher.

We are two scarecrows: sacks and hay;
nodding toward eternity, we tip toward clay.

Blue-veined Old Hands

I never saw them coming
till they were spread bleak
as the limbs of Winter trees
across vacant heavens.

When I said I loved you
I lashed at the wall
with a stick of oar weed
picked off the strand.

Cantankerous old fool :
never saw him coming
till words I spat out
fell like lightning turned
to twigs of rotten wood.

Soldier

Shot crossing a wasteground;
they left him,
pockets pilfered,
staring beyond all wars;

a trail of photographs
and letters running from him
like a congealed flow
of memories.

Before The End

The bedside lamp shone
in the pool of her eye,
made her teeth translucent,
runnelled her face.

Daylight and I were reluctant visitors.
The room, smelling of trapped breath,
sickness and decay, made me anxious
that I would inhale her disease;

and all I loved gone;
all dwindled down to duty.

Armani Stops at our House

Ferrari
sunbathing on the verge,

Armani
surveyed from the wall.

Rolex
grinning up a cuff,

Nikon
stole granddad's gappy smile.

Ray-bans
snapping the moment shut,

Gucci
stepped from the grass;

Pirelli
spat dust into our gateway.

The Yellow Rose
for Alan Biddle (1952-1994).

When his eyes had shut for good
and his face was just a face
and conversation had slowed
to the ebb and flow of memories
speaking among themselves,
a small gesture recast the day.
She placed a yellow rose on his chest
over the picture of the Sacred Heart.
The gentleness of that moment;

the single rose: how well chosen;
how well she chose it.
His face changed, full of ease
as through all his illness,
but death had sculpted warmth away.
His eyes shut against us,
fingers tangled up in rosary beads;
I'll remember him alive
or remember the rose when he was dead.

Legend

Though birds have nested
among the thorns, and the trunk
has grown wild with ivy,

his arms and legs
are still outlined in those sinews,
his belly is a knot of growth.

Deep in the withered leaves
shines an eye; a fish swims there;
he who eats the fish lives forever.

They say he was nailed to the tree,
well above the ground
so a soldier could lance his side

to satisfy the crowds
that fish swim in rivers,
wishes swim in blood.

Coping. Not Coping

You screamed; no one was listening; you wondered
if you had screamed at all.

I asked where those lines on your face came from;
another line appeared.

Now, because your eyes are perpetually electrocuted,
I talk and talk;

always taking the precaution of being somewhere else
before stopping.

Screenplay

1.
I watched the film on her face;
settled into that landscape

of shadows flitting, as images
scudded across the screen.

I could spend a lifetime
beneath that sky;

grow old like a fisherman
whose eyes are burnished

from watching weather;
his face tattooed from living it.

2.
He thinks I do not notice;
he never once looked at the screen.

But wrapped up snug in his feather down gaze
I was electricity,

played the film on my face
so he could read inside me,

and then, if he liked what he saw,
he would be mine.

In sickness there was only you

light as a feather,
relieved of the weight
of position and pride;

neither bluff nor brashness
nor the strength
to be more than your dying self.

Who Knows

what shaped a face,
curled a mouth,
hollowed cheeks,
darkened eye-sockets;

why a voice faltered:
what words said,
hope snapped,
memory snagged.

There are no answers;
only the trickle of blood
through the four
chambers of the heart.

*Last Tuesday Fabulous Arthur Quinn
was Found Dead in his House.*

Fabulous Arthur Quinn
and His Rhythm Fountain,
Cloudland, 1967.

They saw the advertisement
in the Roscommon Herald.
It was in a box under the bed.

The Fountain must have dried up
quickly; Arthur worked
in the meat factory for years.

Left with a broken wrist in 1983
and went home,
he can't have been that old.

They said Fabulous Arthur
must have stared at his ceiling
for at least 6 days without blinking.

Visit

When I am sleeping
you come
softly over these stones;
I turn deeper.
You slip words into my ears,
liquid syllables,
sickles sliding down.

Night-time turns drunk;
longing for more,
your tongue to enwrap me;
I turn deeper.
You trickle down dreams;
our limbs braided,
we slip into one.

Frost in Dublin

Suddenly sycamore branches
were fissures in the porcelain sky,

question marks hung like apparitions
above cows at a barbed wire fence,

rusted tins and abandoned nests
were the exposed secrets of blackberry bushes,

white grass stood
stiffer than cats' whiskers,

birdsong spilled down
from God knows where;

and the earth beneath my feet,
was more magnificent than all the palaces
that ever sparkled in my sleep.

Looking For Your Boat

Looking for your boat on the sea;
my eyes: spotlights
trawling
the emptiness.

Wider;
my eyes,
big as cinema screens,
scanning the ocean.

Wider still;
skies swallowing;
but still it was
not there.

Too wide;
looking into the Gulf of Mexico;
and, all the time, you
were seeing everything

Please Turn Your Head Mr Kavanagh

Look at the canal:
all bronze, copper and gold;
a treasure chest poured
at your feet
this third last evening of December

Contemplating one square foot of water,
albeit black as Guinness,
while the western sky is ablaze:
Mr Kavanagh, the universe
has unfurled for you.

Horse-drawn carriages and taxis slow
on Wilton Terrace:
they point you out Mr Kavanagh;
commemoration indeed,
and the gold slipping from the water.

Growing Apart — A Separation

You take the sea, I'll take the land.
Growing cautious in air currents
my ears will extend to points,
my nose grow long, eyes flinty.
I will have hair to thwart the wind,
jointed limbs that angle to take a fall.

Your sides will be sleek to cut the water,
your face an arrow, even eye-lids
planed to nothing. Your skin
will have the dapples of flowing liquid,
drop-shaped scales. By then, of course,
we will not recognize each other at all.

Outside Tesco's

Her hand is tracing a face:
she sees it where her fingertips are
brushing down the cheek,
following along the jaw,
sweeping off the chin.

And then, it seems,
she doesn't see it any more.
Standing outside Tesco's,
tears flowing down her cheeks,
distraught at this sudden disappearance.

At Naomh Einne's Well

Kneeling down, the jacket off,
shirt sleeves rolled to the oxter,
he slipped his arm into the water,
scooped out the price of a pint,
then thought the better of it
and decided he'd have two.

Then again the following Tuesday
and the following Tuesday too
till there were only clear circles
and coppers on the green bottom,
a bowl in a gap in the wall,
a cross in another with a ladder
of matchsticks and thread.

Sure Sight

I see
pearl-like
dawn
in
your face

a desolate
blue
yonder
in
your irises

the wash
of slivered
moonlight
in
your smile

I know of
nowhere
less trodden
more
perfect

I contract
to be
forever
an explorer
in that universe

There,

laid out on water;
preserved to sharpness in the December chill.

Fluid mosaic of sky and cloud,
Michael shivers like a flag.

Evening, extinguishing the bog cotton,
will find him alone,

treading visions in this bog hole's bottomless black.

Then and Now

Light cavorting on the stream,
choruses of flies on dung,
the flush green of Roscommon fields.

Whole afternoons I would spend
watching minnows dart
beneath those smidereens of sunlight.

Larder to larder, cold flowing weed,
combed fresh opulence.
No trickery in a jam jar; dull brown they died.

This morning sitting in Dublin;
smidereens of sunlight played on the ceiling
and I remembered this.

Railway Child

Picking wood splinters
from my clothes,

ear to the track
and the soft thunder

of a train hurrying
from Ballymurray.

Day, a gift across
a stretch of line,

was measured
in disappearing trains

and struck on coinage
with the flattening of pennies.

Thunder Shower

I wanted you to love me
so much, my mind aged
with the longing.

I was lugging that dried
stump of disappointment
when the shower poured down.

A million light bulbs smashed,
a succession of tungsten roars,
sheets and prongs of lightning.

That's what it took; suddenly
I collapsed, a bawl of laughter
on the Rathmines Road.

Cruise Missiles

Jesus, the padre prayed,
direct these missiles onto the heads
of our enemies.

Except that's not what he said. He said
we pray that these missiles will be efficient
in their function.

Then. Up Jesus,
ride them clean down their throats.
Except, of course, he didn't say that either;

but blessed them with holy water.
After that, the missiles were dispatched,
American missionaries to Europe.

Fifteen Irises from my Black Humour to You

The mallards go off like a shot gun;
each a storm of wings
and black as a keyhole.

The pond, empty now,
is gripped in a glacial sulk.

Fifteen irises from my black humour to you,
their shadows only;
the pond will part with no more.

When you pass

cups miss mouths,
ladders slip,
buckets crash down,

cars veer,
cyclists swerve,
drunkards sober up,

poles and policemen collide,
business men miss kerbs,
schoolboys drool.

Me? I'm just your wing mirror,
enjoying the devastation
behind you.

Old Man

The tyre hanging in the garden
is proof that children used to play there;
but in the breeze it's a shaking head.

Today snowflakes flying by
leave the sycamore white on its northern side.
The garden is still: no snowman, no footprints.

The tyre is an old man;
with an old voice he explains
"I cannot remember names; truth is

I hung too close to the trunk to be of use;
the sycamore branches bolted upwards;
to this day they've never spread out."

Revisiting Lough Ree

Morning comes colourless;
trees stoop to the lake like pilgrims
witnessing images that are riddles in the water.

A sudden shriek: "Over here, no here, over here."
I see nothing; the lake keeps its children chilled
in ice buckets among the reeds.

Once I trailed a ripple from a boat
that bevelled this water. I'll remember the oars'
loud soft thud, slap till I die.

It was June. Insects teemed on the surface.
The sun, that tanned our backs, lulled the countryside
into sleep before the fields were even cranked.

My father was there.

Now December. The lake drags its cutlery
through this cress-green landscape
with an indifference that leaves memories shivering.

Wish

On days like this trees shine,
leaves spill light,
the garden is a flood,
rooftops are full-flowing weirs.
I am swept along.

You, who collect sunlight
on the spatulas of your fingers
(it clings to you like pollen),
curl a hand upward
to loosen out your hair;

Oh, I wish my eyes were barrels.

Running Away

He ran in his Sunday clothes across Casey's field, past Bully's
Acre, out over the line to the tree above the stream. Climbed it
and sat all afternoon among the leaves' shivery dampness, on
frozen branches, under clouds bulging rain.

With crab-apples falling, dumbed time, to the grass below, he
promised he'd stay there forever. Let them come, swarm
beneath the tree, he'd not breathe; no matter how they called, he
would not answer. He composed a poem :

> There is a place for me
> up among the branches
> of a crab-appled lord,
> ivy-draped; golden treasures
> mix with stars of leaves.

> There inside the elbow
> with autumn breezes
> close by shoulder,
> quiet as an owl,
> I long to be.

But two hours later, when the houses' yellow windows were
calling tea-time across the fields, sorrel leaves and crab apples
were promising a particularly sour tomorrow; since he was very
hungry, he went home.

Those Marches

When they play those marches
and the drums tip away,

I think of Brendan,
alone in his sitting room,
flicking channels,
news to news;
dinners collecting on the table.

When they play those marches
and the drums tip away,

I think of Peter
who hated cameras;
his reflection
in the mirror
between the bottles.

When they play those marches
and the drums tip away

I think of Tom
who asked for a present
on his death bed;
I didn't have one,
no one else came.

When they play those marches
and the drums tip away

I think of John
who asked me to visit,

gentlest man
I've ever known;
I didn't.

When they play those marches,
play those marches;
when they play those marches,
the drums tip away.

Explorers
Poem for Elaine

Then, I was the explorer
with that pedal happiness in my feet;
down a tunnel of laurels
or wellington-deep in water.

Now I have to be reminded:
there are furze trails to be charted,
tracking to be done in the tall grass,
and we should be deadly quiet
in the hedge caverns after dark.

Angry

Among the blocks of the establishment
a flawless rise bolted your trust;

success was cement,
all loose notions were pebble-dashed.

Now you revise:
the establishment, its self-righteous system:

how many bodies like you
have fallen from the sides to point the pyramid?

And how many times did you skate over principles,
that I remember, you once held dearly?

Trap

I was in a hawthorn,
trapped in its branches;
all arms, hands and fingers
prevailing on me not to struggle.

I was an exhibit in a jar
ragged and shock-eyed,
praying for a passer-by
where ravens perch still for hours.

I was a storm-blown tatter
caught in another's stitching;
my cries drifting into the sky
nonchalant like dandelion seeds.

Snowtime

Snow:
a million spiders
climbing down.

You cried and cried;
nothing could hold back
whatever pushed
the water from your eyes.

I turned my mind over
so many times,
spoke with every voice I could;
it was nothing.

But why snow?

Seeing...

(part of my love story)

discarded matches on the pub floor,
reflections in gutters,
cobwebs in the corners of ceilings,
petals shed and shriveling,
railings' wrought iron curlicues,
broken windows, tattered curtains,
carrier bags snagged on branches,
the moon running along beside me,
heron one-legged by the pond,
a glove on the footpath ;

each fleck, speck, flaw in your argument;
every minute branded, second burned
as thoroughly as a pipe smoker's match.

Suddenly...
(in memory of Michael Martin)

the stack of papers in the staff room belongs to the past,
the word 'remember' keeps cropping up in our conversations
with the cream cakes, jacket pockets lined with biros,
floppy discs abandoned beside the computer.

Suddenly our memories are linked. A day will come
when one of us meeting another on a street will say
"Do you remember ?" and be answered "Yes. Yes, I do."
and for a moment the two will be one.

Suddenly "enjoy your summer" also means
"come back well. It matters."
And some I would wish to kiss good-bye,
for our shared past, for the times we are one.

Galileo

My mother's china cracked
because of that blue;
a brittle blue.

Your eyes are blood-shot :
bolts of lightening
crack your gaze.

Sitting at this round sky's
centre I can gauge
the universe's balance.

Your irises;
for an hour, two, three,
I am Galileo.

In Memory of Kathleen

Death played you on the end of his line;
you, like that fish, with the old hooks
in your mouth.

Today, landed, truth is there won't be
many admiring the gleam of your body
on the hospital bed

nor the staunchness in your eye.
The struggle wore that away.
But they'll admire the fight, and

in your acquiescence remember
the brilliance of your pride,
your defiance in sickness and health.

Frosty Morning From My Parents Bedroom

The music box plays
my mother's glass-topped
mahoganey
dressing table;

the frost-petalled
window
with a peep hole
for my blue eye;

a hedge of brittle
looping briars,
Curley's field a flood
of sugary brilliance;

the beeches,
their heads in the stratosphere;
a barbed-wire fence
straggling between them;

abbey ruins,
a spire and steeple:
Roscommon town
cocooned beside

an ocean of duck egg blue
that rolls into a bay
beneath snowy mountains
a million miles away.

Low

Counted the stools,
studied marks on the wood,
examined the shoes,
took particular interest in a pair of crutches,
a white cardigan,
observed everyone that passed through,
the organisation of every seating arrangement,
read all the beer mats
read the Becks ad over and over,
thought up a few lines:

"dry stone,
 a rock amid swirling conversations."

Where The Poetry Comes From

Fathomless blue;
Blue sky.

Two swallows proclaiming it
Are extravagant

Dancers in an empty ballroom.
A church bell chimes

Two, three, five o' clock;
No matter;

Tracing curves endlessly;
A route to south Africa ?

Fathomed true;
Blue sky.

Moonfire

If only you'd come,
seen the moonfire on the mountains,
the granite glowing underfoot,
the cream grass shining.

And those clouds like flames
whipped from the mountain-top
with the moon's alabaster whiteness
trapped, a prisoner inside them.

And I wish you'd seen me
with the mad swirl of a kite
lashing songs into the wind
beyond the city's iodine stain.

Films in Your Face

I am watching the film in your face:
your enjoyment crinkling
at the corners of your eyes,
teeth catching your lower lip,
blood draining from the pressure,
draining back as soon.

Furrows on your forehead,
I am smiling at your absorption,
want to stub them out with my thumb
but you catch me looking
so I turn back to the screen
till your face is mine again.

The words on my lips
remain unsaid. There will a time
when, not having words,
I will wish I had spoken; a time
when love being tested, I could say
I used to watch films in your face.

The Poems are Past

The poems are past;
goodnight, au revoir.

And life, handed over like a cheque;
good luck, all the best.

Still: an adjective for a man ?
Still?

Think of rain bucketing down,
sunshine caught in its strings;

that's how I think of you:
a rainstorm in June: gentle subversive.

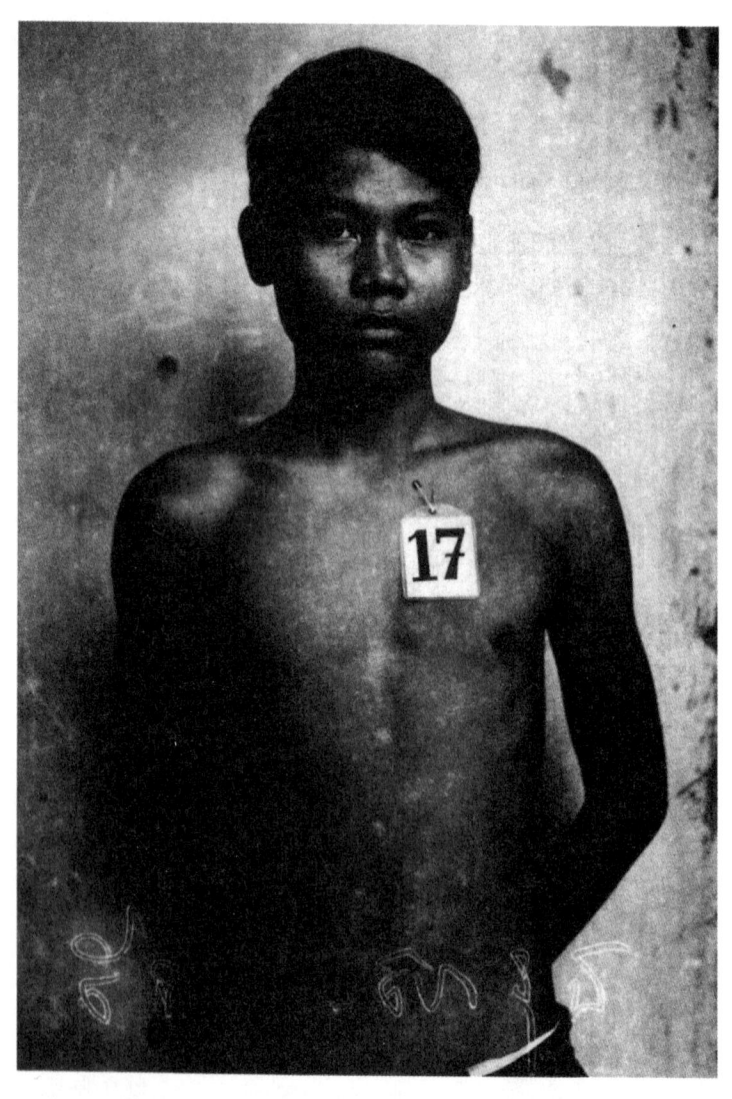

from "The Killing Fields", Chris Riley and Douglas Niven;
copyright 1996 Twin Palms Publishers, New Mexico;
www.twinpalms.com

Tuol Sleng Still

[Introduction

In 1999 I chanced upon "The Killing Fields" (Twin Palms Publishers), a collection of 78 photographs of prisoners from the archive of Tuol Sleng Museum of Genocide, previously Tuol Sleng prison. Between 1975 and 1979 fourteen thousand people were incarcerated there, previously a secondary school in Phnom Penh; only seven survived.

The faces in these photographs convey, with the greatest power, the sadness that is visited upon victims of war. I was compelled to consider, more deeply than I had hitherto, the primitiveness of war, of ourselves that resort to it over and over.

Each poem in the series was suggested by a particular face. I make no claims for the authenticity of my interpretations. Nor do I imagine the poems add to the strength of the emotions the photographs stir. They are an attempt to bring the experience closer to myself, by imagining what these peoople might have been thinking. I also wanted to pass on details of the background to these photographs.

Most of the prisoners were wearing tag numbers. In some cases there were no tag numbers. They were male and female, some very old, some babies in their mothers' arms. It seems a long time ago now, and yet the youngest would be in their mid-twenties if they were alive.]

1

Once my father and I found a skull
in a field with the hum of a bee inside.
My father said it was a last thought,
that a man's last thought stays forever
in his head.

I didn't want to touch the skull,
just to move closer to see a last thought;
but as I did the bee flew out and I ran
terror-stricken back to my father;
horrified for having tipped the natural order.

2

"Work hard," my father used say,
"Work hard and you'll owe nobody."
I worked hard in Battambang,

in the cooperative there,
kept my mouth shut, head down;
but that was not enough.

Spies perched under our eye-lids,
nested in our ears; even as we slept
we had to gag the heroes in our dreams.

His advice was somewhere in my head;
they found it and I was convicted:
a man with a strategy for being free.

3

We left the field to find food;
that was treason.
There were ten of us on the truck,
tied hands to feet;

we were not told our destination;
I thought there was none.
When we arrived at the prison we heard
the screams from behind closed windows.

Beaten to the ground again,
I curled up so small
that I made them a football
and they kicked it senseless.

Every day people disappear;
all of a sudden they are gone
like casual labourers that move on quietly.
But here a disappearance is photographed.

4

From today I am 85.

More usable,
fileable,
flexible.
Forgettable,
losable,
reprintable.

5

My face has crumbled under the weight
of my child's incomprehension.

He knows fear but not evil,
has not learned that men wield
the power to remove the light
by which he knows himself;

that the goodness I've planted
ends at this gunpoint.

6

I had plans to leave our farm,
to go to Phnom Penh;
but they emptied Phnom Penh
like you'd empty a room.

Whole streets cleared,
peoples' lives cleared,
sent away to farm;
not a farmer among them.

One night I argued the sense of this,
argued with a friend;
I said not everyone is a farmer,
just as well.

My friend passed on the message;
they said I've listened too much;
but still I say to myself,
not everyone is a farmer.

7

When 40 is slipped into the file after 39
I will have no position in the world
but will be just another screaming
in the darkness of Tuol Sleng.

I'm so conscious of this number,
its weightlessness on my chest :
my death certificate hanging
from an open safety-pin.

8

Looking away from the camera, I see
two soldiers hacking a prisoner's legs
till he's on his knees; the next is waiting
for his shins to explode into pain.

Ten-year olds screaming instructions,
angel-faces with AK-47s;
childhoods manured in hatred
leaning against our horizon.

In twelve hours I've seen so much
I'm staring through it.
A lifetime scratches down that glass;
my mind is overrun with atrocities.

9

It is not enough that you die,
but you keep company with death;
tethered to it, in all its stages.

I am nineteen;
by starvation and torture, in a month,
I'll be seventy.

And men hold guardianship of this:
delivering more plagues
than would rage over a millennium.

Fear is churning snakes in my belly;
there is no side-stepping this future;
we are marched single-file into it.

10

And my child?
He sleeps with barely more than birth's darkness in his head.

I watch his famine coming as surely as a train;
but make no mistake, if you see fear, it is fear of the void
at the centre of my child's screams for food.

All else is contempt for men who cultivate dreams
where his will never grow.

11

I looked at him,
Cambodian like myself,
similar in height and age.
He was handing out the tags;
I was bare to the waist.

I held the tag in my hand,
holding it up to be seen;
feeling awkward, conspicuous.
"Pin it onto your chest"
he said and waited.

I pinned it into my skin;
the humiliation delighted him.
Before the camera I stood erect
like I was proud to wear it,
like it was made of gold.

12

One morning in 1973 I woke up in a tunnel of noise
beneath a sky of crosses, B-52s coming over;
turned our village into hell.
My father didn't come home that day, nor the next.
They collected the bodies from the fields;
he was found beside our fallen ox.
We were too young;
nobody told us.

One morning my mother told me to run to my cousin's.
She pushed me away. She screamed at me. So I ran.
It was a long way. With my heart bursting and legs
collapsing, I fell in the door with no story to tell
but my mother's screaming. That's how I remember her:
screaming, pushing me. That's how I've come to understand
'no information'.

13

Let them flash my hatred,
let it pierce them;
if they dislike it, they can kill me;
they will anyway.

Be sure lens, don't miss my steady eye
and fixed mouth;
know that every muscle in my body
is a clenched fist.

14

I will not look up.
I will not allow them look
me in the eye.

The light that shines there
I control;
I will not comply.

Though freedom be reduced
to the thimble-full,
I'll have it when I die.

15

My mother was led away
roped to fifteen others.
By chance I was there, within ten metres,
unable to speak, to nod, to touch.
Mother, my betrayal haunts me,
I sit through the early hours
begging your forgiveness.

And I see the glance
warning me not to know you
again and again.
It is eternity that frightens me;
an eternity in which you will not see
your love returned.